Original title:
The Frozen Dream

Copyright © 2024 Swan Charm
All rights reserved.

Author: Swan Charm
ISBN HARDBACK: 978-9916-79-387-9
ISBN PAPERBACK: 978-9916-79-388-6
ISBN EBOOK: 978-9916-79-389-3

Twilight in the Frosted Pines

In twilight's glow, the pines stand tall,
Frosty coats glisten, a winter call.
Shadows dance in the fading light,
Nature whispers, bidding goodnight.

Silvery beams through branches weave,
In this calm, dreams softly conceive.
A blanket of stillness cloaks the ground,
In the air, magic and peace abound.

The Stillness of Chilling Night

The night is deep, silence profound,
Snowflakes swirl, softly they sound.
Stars twinkle like secrets untold,
In the hush of winter, night unfolds.

Breath of frost on every face,
Nature rests in tranquil grace.
Moonlight kisses the frozen stream,
Life is quiet; we drift in dream.

Velvet Frost on Broken Dreams

Frost covers fields like a tender embrace,
Whispers of hope in the quiet space.
Dreams long lost in a soft winter's chill,
Awakened by stillness, the heart learns to feel.

Velvet touches the edges of night,
Restoring the hopes once lost from light.
In every crystal, a story stays,
Of battles fought in forgotten days.

Winter's Breath on Slumbering Seeds

Winter's breath whispers soft and low,
Nurturing seeds concealed beneath snow.
In the heart of frost, potential lies,
Awaiting the sun to rise in the skies.

Dreams of blossoms beneath the cold,
Silent promises yet untold.
Nature's cycle, a timeless dance,
In stillness, awaits spring's advance.

Celestial Chill

The stars above, they glimmer bright,
A blanket of frost, a stunning sight.
Whispers of night through pine trees weave,
In the silence deep, the world takes leave.

Moonlight dances on icy streams,
Wrapped in the hush of winter dreams.
Chill in the air, breath forms a mist,
Nature's embrace, too warm to resist.

Every flake falls with grace divine,
Painting the earth in silver line.
Under the canopy, calm and still,
The heart beats softly, the void we fill.

Frosted Footprints in the Mind

Memories linger like footprints in snow,
Fading with time, yet they still glow.
Each step we take, a story untold,
In the chill of silence, warmth to behold.

Winding paths through the cold, crisp air,
Echoes of laughter, floating everywhere.
Etched in my heart, the moments we shared,
In the frost, a testament of how we cared.

Glances exchanged beneath the pale moon,
Promises sealed, our own sweet tune.
Frosted memories, never erased,
In the labyrinth of time, forever embraced.

Illusions Adrift in the Snow

Drifting like dreams in the winter white,
Phantoms of warmth in the hush of night.
Whispers of hope on a cold, breezy air,
Illusions dance lightly, without a care.

Shapes in the snow, visions take flight,
Fleeting like shadows in pale moonlight.
Nature's own canvas, ever so grand,
Falls into silence, gently unplanned.

With every snowfall, thoughts intertwine,
A tapestry woven in frosty design.
Holding the echoes of laughter and sighs,
In this frozen world, where dreams never die.

Tales from the Glacial Depths

Under the ice, where shadows lie,
Ancient tales whisper, as time slips by.
Murky and deep, secrets entombed,
In the glacial embrace, history loomed.

Each crack in the surface tells a story,
Of love and loss, of faded glory.
In the depths of the glacier, silence reigns,
Hiding the echoes of forgotten pains.

Frozen fragments of lives once lived,
In the stillness and chill, what nature gives.
Under layers of ice, old worlds collide,
In the mysteries held where the past must bide.

Crystalized Aspirations

In the heart of a dream,
A spark begins to glow,
With each hope we gather,
Our future starts to show.

Like crystals in the light,
Shining bright and pure,
Every wish we whisper,
Opens a new door.

Through the frost we journey,
On paths unknown to all,
Each step brings us closer,
To the dreams that call.

We'll break the chains of doubt,
With courage intertwined,
Our aspirations crystal,
In our hearts enshrined.

So let us chase these visions,
With spirits bold and free,
For in this world of ice,
Our dreams will flourish, see.

Frosted Visions

In the still of the dawn,
When the world wears a glaze,
Frosted visions linger,
In a delicate haze.

The trees stand adorned,
With icy lace and gleam,
Whispering secrets soft,
Of a wintry dream.

As the breath of the night,
Leaves a fog in the air,
We follow the glimmers,
With a heart full of prayer.

Each sparkle a promise,
Of beauty to unveil,
In the realm of the quiet,
Where wonders never pale.

With every crisp footstep,
A new story unfolds,
In the realm of frost,
Where magic gently holds.

Chill of Wistful Nights

Under a silver moon,
The chill wraps around,
Wistful dreams take flight,
In silence profound.

The stars, like whispers,
Share tales of the past,
In the depths of night,
Our memories are cast.

A breath on the window,
Leaves patterns of grace,
In the coolness of shadows,
We find our own place.

With each fleeting moment,
We hold on tight, yet light,
To the chill of these nights,
Where our hearts take flight.

As dawn slowly breaks,
Wistful thoughts drift away,
But the chill lingers on,
In the light of the day.

Enchanted in Ice

In a realm filled with wonder,
Where the cold winds sigh,
We stand enchanted here,
'Neath a wintering sky.

The beauty of the frost,
Wraps the world in a glow,
Each flake a tiny story,
In the whispers of snow.

Glistening like the stars,
On the canvas of night,
We dance in the silence,
With hearts full of light.

Embraced by the stillness,
In the world made of dreams,
Each moment enchanted,
In the soft, silver beams.

So let the ice surround us,
In the magic we find,
For in this frozen moment,
Our souls are intertwined.

Glacial Mists of Memory

Whispers float within the frost,
A time suspended, echoes lost.
In shadows deep where silence dwells,
Memory's grip, a fragile spell.

Frosted breath upon the glass,
Moments captured, moments pass.
A world once bright, now dimmed by chill,
The heart recalls against its will.

Icicles weep from ancient stone,
Tales of warmth in winter's throne.
Behind each flake a story hides,
In glacial mists, the past resides.

Silent screams in frozen air,
Fleeting joy, but none can share.
Reflections shimmering like stars,
Beneath the weight of icy bars.

Yet perhaps in this frozen night,
A spark of hope, a distant light.
For every flurry, every sigh,
Reminds us how the past can fly.

Ephemeral Dreams in a Snowglobe

Within the sphere, a world confined,
A fleeting dream, a dance defined.
Snowflakes swirl in gentle grace,
A moment held in time and space.

Each shake reveals a winter scene,
Of joy, of laughter, soft and keen.
Yet time can steal what it bestows,
The crystal globe, it comes and goes.

Figures dance beneath the dome,
Whispers soft, a fragile home.
But outside waits the cold and grey,
An endless night that steals away.

In dreamy realms, we find our glee,
As snowflakes fall, we dream to be.
Yet precious dreams can fade so fast,
In snowglobe worlds, we cannot last.

So cherish time within that sphere,
A fleeting glimpse, a moment dear.
For when it's shattered, like our dreams,
We'll realize all is not as it seems.

An Odyssey in the Ice

Through endless white, the wanderer strides,
A heart of fire, where hope abides.
The tundra whispers secrets low,
In frozen grips, the cold winds blow.

Footprints trailing in the deep,
Lost in thoughts, where shadows creep.
Amongst the glaciers' towering might,
The soul ignites to seek the light.

With every breath, the icy air,
A test of will, a silent prayer.
The stars above, they guide the way,
Through frigid nights and endless day.

A journey forged in winter's womb,
Where dreams arise, and fears consume.
Yet in the silence, answers call,
An odyssey, we rise or fall.

And when at last the dawn breaks free,
With colors bright, a majesty.
We find a path through ice and fire,
In every step, our hearts desire.

Chronicles of the Cold

In shadows cast by pale moonlight,
The chronicles unfold at night.
A tale of winter's icy breath,
Of life entwined with whispered death.

Beneath each layer of the snow,
Hidden stories from long ago.
Frozen tears and secrets kept,
In silence deep where silence wept.

Branches bare against the sky,
Echoes of dreams that dared to fly.
Candles flicker, shadows sway,
The cold reveals what words can't say.

With every storm, a story stirs,
In howling winds, a voice concurs.
The frost will etch its timeless mark,
Each chapter bright, each phrase a spark.

In chronicles where hearts are bold,
Through winter's grasp, the truth unfolds.
For in the cold, we learn to be,
The keepers of our legacy.

Frozen Echoes

In the stillness of the night,
Whispers dance in icy air,
Footsteps linger, then take flight,
Carried forth, without a care.

Stars above, they gently gleam,
Casting shadows on the ground,
Where silence wraps its quiet dream,
In this place, lost souls are found.

Crystal branches sway with grace,
Reflecting all the light they hold,
Time stands still in this embrace,
Stories waiting to be told.

Echoes wander through the trees,
Singing songs from long ago,
Carried softly by the breeze,
In this world of ice and snow.

Frosty breath, a fleeting trace,
Reminds us of what once was near,
In frozen echoes we find space,
To remember all we hold dear.

Shards of a Snowy Slumber

Snowflakes fall like whispered dreams,
Covering all in gentle white,
Nature sleeps in softest beams,
Wrapped in warmth, embraced by night.

Underneath the frozen skin,
Life awaits with patient grace,
Hopes and wishes deep within,
In quietude, they find their place.

Branches bow with crystal weight,
Shards of ice that glimmer bright,
Each a wish we dare to state,
Floating softly into night.

Moonlight dances on the ground,
Painting shadows, silvered glow,
In this silence, peace is found,
In dreams of winter's gentle flow.

When the thaw begins to rise,
All awaits a new rebirth,
From slumber's hold, the spirit flies,
As springtime whispers of its worth.

The Quiet Chill of Yearning

In the chill of evening's breath,
Longing seeps into the night,
A longing deep as whispered death,
Filling hearts with silent fright.

Frosted glass, a window frame,
Keeps the warmth of memory,
Names once spoken, now like flame,
Flicker soft in quiet plea.

Yearning dances through the air,
A tender ache that lingers long,
Shadows speak of love and care,
In the night, they sing their song.

Stars above, they flicker soft,
Guiding hearts to dreams untold,
In the stillness, spirits loft,
Chasing warmth through winter's cold.

Yet in the silence, hope will glow,
Through the chill, it finds a way,
For even in the icy flow,
Yearning blooms at break of day.

Glaze of Forgotten Memories

A thin glaze on the window pane,
Holds the ghosts of times gone by,
Fleeting sights of joy and pain,
In its shimmer, shadows lie.

Underneath the sparkling frost,
Memories pulse, alive, yet dim,
Every loss and every cost,
Wrapped in whispers, soft and slim.

Footprints fade in sheets of white,
Marking moments lost in time,
Echoes drift, they take their flight,
Carrying with them a rhyme.

In the glaze, reflections gleam,
Stories buried in the past,
All the bittersweet and dream,
Held in stillness, ever last.

Yet as the thaw begins to break,
Memories dance in warming light,
With every crack, new paths we take,
Embracing day, embracing night.

The Icebound Reverie

Amidst the shimmering snow,
Reflections dance in twilight's glow.
Silent whispers fill the air,
In this dreamlike, cold affair.

Frosty blooms on windows cling,
While the frozen echoes sing.
Crisp and chill, the world feels near,
In the heart, my dreams appear.

Snowflakes twirl like graceful sprites,
In the stillness of the nights.
A canvas white, unmarked, so wide,
Where fantasies and shadows hide.

Morning breaks with tender light,
Melting dreams of starry night.
With every breath, the frost will fade,
Yet in my heart, the magic stayed.

Lost in time, this reverie,
Cradled in tranquility.
A world untouched by winter's hand,
Where hope and dreams forever stand.

Wandering Through Frigid Poles

Through the icy wilderness,
Where shadows gather, cold caress.
A solitary path I trace,
Wandering through this frozen space.

Whispers of the ancient ice,
Every step, a silent price.
Glistening crystals on the floor,
Hold secrets of the tales of yore.

The aurora paints the skies,
In vibrant shades, the spirit flies.
Upon the breath of winter's air,
I find a song hidden somewhere.

Mountains high, the glaciers gleam,
In the stillness, lost in dream.
Each breath a cloud, I pause to see,
What mysteries the cold holds for me.

Endless night, a tranquil peace,
In the frozen depths, I find release.
Wandering 'neath the stars so bright,
In this frigid world, pure delight.

Fractured Fragments of Frost

Shattered glimmers on the ground,
Silent echoes all around.
Frosted whispers in the breeze,
Nature's art, with graceful ease.

The windows weep with crystal tears,
Reflecting tales of distant years.
In every shard, a story's told,
Of winters past, of brave and bold.

Icicles hang like swords of glass,
Time stands still as moments pass.
Carving lines on paths of white,
Fractured pieces, pure delight.

A dance of snowflakes in the air,
Each one unique, beyond compare.
They twirl and spin in chilly gusts,
Building dreams upon the dusts.

In this realm where cold prevails,
Underneath the hushed exhale.
Fractured fragments tell a tale,
Of winter's beauty, soft and frail.

Melodies of Ice and Dream

Songs of frost beneath the stars,
Chiming softly, whispering ours.
In the quiet, dreams arise,
Carved in ice, beneath the skies.

Glistening echoes fill the night,
Melodies of silver light.
Each note a crystal, clear and bright,
Painting shadows, pure delight.

Windswept plains, a tranquil sea,
Where every breath feels wild and free.
In this realm of frosty grace,
I find a warm, embracing space.

The moonlight kisses frozen streams,
Awakening forgotten dreams.
In the stillness, hearts will soar,
To the rhythm of winter's lore.

As the dawn breaks, light will play,
On the ice, in a golden ray.
Melodies linger in the seam,
Of frozen hope and gentle dream.

A Journey Through Frozen Reveries.

In shadows deep, where ice must sleep,
The whispers chill, a haunting thrill.
Across the frost, lost dreams are tossed,
In winter's grasp, we dare to clasp.

Amidst the snow, where cold winds blow,
Time stands still, hearts seek their will.
Each step we trace, a frozen grace,
Through silken nights, we find our plight.

The quiet peaks, where silence speaks,
A canvas wide, the dreams reside.
With every breath, we flirt with death,
Embracing fate, we navigate.

In twilight's glow, while moonlight flows,
Reflections gleam, like shattered dreams.
Our spirits soar, through icy lore,
In frozen lands, we make our stands.

As dawn breaks clear, dispelling fear,
A journey planned, through this fair land.
In beauty's clutch, we feel so much,
Within this trance, we take our chance.

Shiver of Whispers

The winds will weave, a tale of eve,
In cold embrace, we find our place.
Each breath a sigh, as shadows fly,
Caught in the frost, we count the cost.

With every chill, our hearts stand still,
A fleeting ghost, the one we boast.
In twilight's glow, the secrets flow,
From lips of ice, a shivering vice.

The silent night, a soft moonlight,
Echoes the fears, held through the years.
With whispers frail, on this white trail,
The past appears, to drench our tears.

In the serene, where stars convene,
We yearn for peace, from this cold fleece.
Yet in the dark, there sparks a spark,
A glimmer bright, to guide our flight.

So let us tread, where dreams are led,
With hearts aglow, through endless snow.
In shivers deep, our souls will leap,
And find a way, to greet the day.

Glacial Reverie

In a world so cold, where stories told,
Of ice and snow, a gentle glow.
The glacial breath, a dance with death,
In quiet lands, we understand.

Each flake that falls, in silence calls,
A memory's thread, where hopes are wed.
The winds will sing, of frozen spring,
In crystal halls, where laughter thralls.

With frozen tears, we fight our fears,
In the icy grip, our spirits slip.
Yet in the dark, there's still a spark,
A flame that glows, beneath the snows.

The nightingale sings, of hidden things,
Across the dome, we find our home.
In moments rare, we shed despair,
And feel the warmth, of love's sweet charm.

So let us dream, on silken streams,
Where light cascades, through glacial shades.
Here in this trance, we take our chance,
And forge our hearts, in winter's dance.

Echoes of Icebound Fantasies

In realms of frost, where dreams are lost,
The echoes call, to one and all.
Through darkened skies, where hope still flies,
We chase the glow, of those we know.

With every breath, we conquer death,
In frozen frames, we carve our names.
The whispers soar, through icy lore,
In shimmers bright, we find our light.

Through lonely nights, our spirit fights,
In shadows cast, memories last.
With every cry, beneath the sky,
We seek the way, to break the gray.

The tales unfold, of hearts so bold,
In this embrace, we find our place.
With dreams as sails, through snowy trails,
We journey forth, to claim our worth.

So let them speak, the winds so meek,
Of love and fear, and those held dear.
With glances cast, we'll hold them fast,
In echoes deep, our dreams shall leap.

Dreams Encased in Ice

Whispers of winter haunt the night,
Silent wishes tucked in tight.
Glistening visions, a fragile thread,
Frozen hopes where shadows tread.

Icicles like tears on branches cling,
Silent echoes of what spring will bring.
Caught in stillness, time stands still,
Chasing warmth through frosted chill.

Reflections dance on a crystal lake,
Memories shimmer, yet softly break.
The heart's desire, a breath away,
Encased in ice till skies turn gray.

In each flake, a dream reborn,
Awakening light at the break of dawn.
With the thaw comes a tender sigh,
In the warmth, our spirits fly.

So let the cold be a gentle guide,
For within the ice, our dreams abide.
In the stillness, we find our grace,
Unraveled hopes in winter's embrace.

When Stars Freeze in Silence

Beneath a dome of midnight blue,
Stars once bright, lost from view.
Time stands still, the cosmos sighs,
As hope flickers, and silence lies.

In the vacuum, dreams take flight,
Blinded by the endless night.
Each heartbeat marks a frozen breath,
In the darkness, we dance with death.

Galaxies twirl, yet still they fade,
Echoes of a serenade.
When silence reigns, the world grows small,
In the stillness, we risk it all.

Yet in this void, a spark remains,
A whisper soft, like gentle rains.
For even frozen, stars embolden,
A promise shared, forever golden.

When all is hushed, we cross the line,
Finding life in the frozen spine.
Together we'll warm the silent space,
When stars freeze, still dreams embrace.

The Frosted Path of Hope

Beneath the frost, the earth lies still,
Each step forward, a hopeful thrill.
Nature's canvas, white and pure,
In the chill, our hearts endure.

Along the path, the shadows blend,
Each whispering gust, a faithful friend.
Through samplers of white, we quietly tread,
With dreams as our guide, where faith is fed.

The air is crisp, the world anew,
With every breath, the promise grew.
In the silence, we pause and see,
A future bright, waiting to be.

Icicles hang like dreams on the brink,
Reminding us not to pause and think.
For every winter must yield to spring,
And from the frost, hope takes wing.

So let us walk this frosted trail,
With every heartbeat, we shall not fail.
For even in cold, our spirits coat,
With dreams ignited, we'll find our note.

Slumbering Visions in Aether

In the depths of night, dreams do float,
On wisps of thought, like a silent boat.
Cradled in arms of hazy skies,
Where all is calm and no one cries.

Visions whisper in the still, soft air,
In the realm of slumber, beyond all care.
Stars blink gently, watching close,
As we drift through the ethereal dose.

Beneath the moon's soft, glowing gaze,
Our silent journeys weave a maze.
In shades of blue, dreams intertwine,
Revealing secrets, tender and divine.

Awakening gently, yet bound to sleep,
In the arms of night, our souls must keep.
With every sigh and every breath,
We dance with dreams, defying death.

So let us wander where shadows play,
In this realm where visions sway.
For in this aether, our minds ignite,
Slumbering visions, our hearts take flight.

Permafrost of the Soul

In the silence, where shadows creep,
Frozen whispers, secrets keep.
Memories buried, deep and still,
Time encased in a crystalline chill.

Yearning hearts, unspoken sighs,
Underneath the winter skies.
Layers of frost cover the past,
Echoes linger, haunting, steadfast.

Life's warmth, a distant glow,
In the depths of the icy flow.
Bound in stillness, trapped in time,
Where the heart and the cold entwine.

Frosty chains, yet hope ignites,
In the darkness, a flicker lights.
Awakening dreams buried deep,
The permafrost slowly starts to weep.

Glimmering in the Cold

Stars above, twinkling bright,
Glimmering softly in the night.
Whispers in the chilly breeze,
Wrapped in warmth, beneath the trees.

Moonlit paths guide our way,
In the hush, where shadows play.
Hearts entwined, a dance so bold,
Lost in dreams, we brave the cold.

Snowflakes fall, a gentle kiss,
Enchanting moments, pure bliss.
Every sparkle, a story told,
In this realm of glimmering gold.

Footprints fade in winter's grace,
As we wander, time won't erase.
Hand in hand, through frost we go,
In this magic, we're aglow.

Shimmering Snowflakes of a Daydream

Drifting softly from the sky,
Snowflakes dance like thoughts that fly.
Each unique, a fleeting art,
Capturing dreams within the heart.

Whirling winds, a gentle tease,
Painting landscapes with such ease.
In the hush, a world so bright,
Shimmering snow, a pure delight.

Daydreams float on frosty air,
Moments captured, sweet and rare.
Every flake, a wish unleashed,
In the silence, joy increased.

Nature's canvas, vast and wide,
Hiding wonders, side by side.
In each spark, a story grows,
Shimmering dreams, winter bestows.

Icebound Secrets

Beneath the ice, the secrets sleep,
Voices trapped where shadows weep.
Hidden truths in layers lie,
Waiting for the spring to cry.

Fractured whispers, cold embrace,
Time unveils each frozen trace.
In the depths, the stories hide,
Silent tales that time can't bide.

Crystals form, their beauty stark,
Illuminating the hidden dark.
Each a keeper, silent and still,
Of the past, the heartbreak, the thrill.

As seasons change, they slowly thaw,
Revealing fragments, nature's law.
Shimmering echoes of what once was,
Icebound secrets, frozen because.

Whispers of Icebound Reverie

In twilight's breath, the shadows crawl,
Where dreams are spun, and silence calls.
A frosty veil drapes over night,
Whispers drift, elusive light.

Beneath the stars, the stillness grows,
Frozen hearts, where winter flows.
Each thought adorned in shimmering frost,
A realm of beauty, never lost.

The echoes beckon from afar,
Guiding paths beneath the stars.
Frigid winds, they softly sigh,
In icebound realms, we learn to fly.

Together lost in whispers sweet,
The dance of snow beneath our feet.
Together we find a world anew,
In icebound dreams, our spirits flew.

Yet as the dawn begins to break,
The fragile dreams we dare to make.
Will thaw beneath the warming rays,
In icebound hearts, forever stays.

Glaciers of the Mind

Thoughts cascade like streams of ice,
Engraved in time, both cold and nice.
The silent whispers twist and bend,
In glaciers deep, where dreams transcend.

Each frozen shard, a truth concealed,
In crystal depth, the heart revealed.
Memories dance in glacial hue,
As echoes of the past break through.

Delve into horizons vast and wide,
Where icy landscapes softly glide.
The barren fields of thought remain,
A tranquil place, both sweet and plain.

Reflections shimmer, bright and clear,
In frosted realms, we shed a tear.
Inside the caverns of the mind,
Unraveled tales, so rare to find.

With every step, the world feels new,
Each glacier whispers shades of blue.
In depths unknown, the soul can grow,
In frozen thoughts, time's quiet flow.

Chilling Echoes of Tomorrow

In twilight's grasp, a chill descends,
The world prepares, as daylight ends.
Echoes linger in icy air,
Yet hope remains, a constant flare.

Frosted dreams like candles glow,
A path ahead through winter's snow.
In whispered breaths, the future calls,
Chilling echoes break down walls.

The stars above twinkle with fate,
Each glimmer holds a heart's debate.
In silence, we await the morn,
Where shadows fade and dreams are born.

Each frozen step reveals a way,
To navigate through night to day.
Awake in worlds where silence reigns,
Chilling echoes spark life's veins.

Together we'll defy the cold,
In frozen tales, our hearts unfold.
With every dawn, a chance to grow,
In chilling whispers, we will flow.

Frostbitten Fantasies

Beneath the frost, where memories lie,
Fantasies weave, both low and high.
In whispered notes, the heart shall sing,
As frozen thoughts take off on wings.

With every breath, a misty haze,
In biting winds, we lose our ways.
Yet in the chill, we find our dreams,
Frostbitten truths, like moonlit beams.

The glittering snow, a jewel bright,
Cloaks every sorrow in pure white.
Through wintry paths, our spirits soar,
In frostbitten realms, we crave for more.

Each icy glance, a world anew,
Of dreams that dance in twilight's dew.
A tapestry of silver bright,
In fantasies born of winter's night.

Together we chase through frozen trees,
In frostbitten realms, with purest ease.
With every step, a heart's embrace,
In whispered dreams, we find our place.

Ethereal Cold

In whispers deep, the silence breathes,
The hoarfrost clings to ancient trees.
Moonlight dances on the frozen ground,
In this chill, lost dreams abound.

Stars like diamonds pierce the night,
Each flake of snow, a spark of light.
Shadows stretch, as moments fade,
In ethereal cold, memories wade.

Winds weave tales of long ago,
Through branches bare, the soft winds blow.
A world adorned in icy sheen,
Nature sleeps, serene, unseen.

Glimmers of joy, tinged with sorrow,
Promises held for a brighter tomorrow.
Frozen echoes of laughter past,
In this cold, we hold steadfast.

Yet in this stillness, hope ignites,
As dawn approaches, bringing light.
Ethereal cold may hold the night,
But warmth will come, and hearts take flight.

Dreams Encased in Frost

Within a glass of frozen dreams,
Time stands still, or so it seems.
Each whisper caught in icy breath,
A world awash in quiet death.

Glimpses of light through frosted panes,
Like fleeting joy in silent pains.
Shattered shadows dance and glide,
In dreams encased, our fears reside.

Footprints vanish, swallowed whole,
Underneath winter's icy shoal.
Frosted whispers drift and sigh,
In this realm where hopes may lie.

Silent wishes in frozen air,
Lie suspended, trapped in despair.
Yet in the heart, a spark remains,
Of warmth that flows through loss and gains.

Tales of warmth escape the cold,
In whispered secrets yet untold.
Dreams encased in frost will thaw,
When spring unveils its gentle claw.

Shattered Winter Reflections

On still, dark lakes, the ice arrives,
Where mirrors break and silence thrives.
Each crack a story, sharp and clear,
In shattered winter, truth draws near.

Glimmers dance on fractured glass,
Time stutters, moments seem to pass.
In chilly air where echoes play,
Reflections shift and drift away.

Ghosts of laughter in frozen air,
Fleeting glimpses of joy laid bare.
Beneath the surface, life will stir,
In winter's grasp, our whispers blur.

Yet in the shards, a warmth remains,
Remind us of our timeless gains.
Shattered pieces, beauty found,
In winter's heart, we're all unbound.

As sunlight breaks on icy shore,
A promise whispered, forevermore.
Shattered winter, a canvas bright,
Reflecting hope in soulful light.

Icy Embrace

In the frosty arms of night,
Stars cast shadows, glowing bright.
A world entangled in silver lace,
Finding solace in icy embrace.

Whirlwinds twirl in frozen grace,
Time holds still in this embrace.
Silent whispers wrap around,
In the quiet, warmth is found.

Fern and pine draped in white,
Nature's canvas, pure delight.
Each breath echoes, crisp and clear,
In icy arms, there's naught to fear.

Yet with each dusk, dreams take flight,
Carried forth by the velvet night.
Icy embrace, a fleeting kiss,
In winter's hold, we find our bliss.

As dawn breaks cold upon the land,
Shadows dance, cupped in our hands.
In the chill, a heart that beats,
Icy embrace, where warmth repeats.

Frost's Embrace on Wistful Thoughts

In the hush of morning light,
Whispers of frost take their flight.
Dreams weave through shivering air,
Each breath a chill, tender and rare.

Silent trees wear crystal crowns,
Softly, the world slowly drowns.
In shades of blue and silver gleam,
Echoes of a frost-kissed dream.

Footsteps crunched on icy ground,
In this realm, new warmth is found.
Memories stir in frozen grace,
Each moment a delicate embrace.

Wistful thoughts drift like snowflakes,
In solitude, my heart awakes.
Nature's art paints the dawn bright,
Frost's embrace, a gentle sight.

As shadows dance in morning's glow,
Time whispers secrets we all know.
Underneath this frosty dome,
Wistful hearts are never alone.

Iridescent Frost Upon Awakening

Morning breaks with frosty kiss,
Nature glimmers, pure and bliss.
Iridescent wonders twinkle,
Upon awakening, hearts dimple.

Sunrise paints the world anew,
Brushing landscapes with glittering hue.
Each blade of grass, a jeweled star,
Transforming dreams, both near and far.

Birds whispered tunes from boughs high,
Underneath the vast, azure sky.
Rays of light, a gentle weave,
In the frost, we learn to believe.

Every step, a crisp refrain,
In these still moments, joy remains.
Iridescent frost, a sweet delight,
Filling our souls with purest light.

As day unfolds its whispered charm,
All worries fade, no cause for alarm.
In the beauty of this waking hour,
Frost holds its gentle power.

Reflections in a Frozen Pool

Beneath the sheen of icy glass,
Stillness holds as moments pass.
Reflections dance in crystal bends,
Secrets of life that never ends.

Echoes whisper through the frost,
In this stillness, we count the cost.
Each ripple holds a hidden tale,
A silent message on the gale.

Leaves drift gently, framed in ice,
Nature's canvas, cold and nice.
Mirrored skies in hues of gray,
Guide our thoughts, both light and stray.

In the depths of this frozen view,
We see ourselves, both old and new.
Reflective thoughts like bubbles rise,
In the calm, truth never lies.

As time hangs still, we learn to ponder,
In the quiet, we grow fonder.
Reflections shimmer in the swoon,
A frozen pool beneath the moon.

The Subtle Dance of Winter's Wish

Softly spins the snowy flake,
In the hush, the world does wake.
Winter whispers, quiet and low,
In each flurry, love does flow.

Branches sway in a gentle breeze,
Draped in white with utmost ease.
Cold hands clasp against the chill,
In winter's grasp, time stands still.

The subtle dance of every flake,
Plays along the frozen lake.
Harmony in the crisp, cold air,
A song of winter, sweet and rare.

Footprints mark the path ahead,
Through snowy realms, where dreams are fed.
Each twirl and swirl a silent wish,
In this moment, hearts truly bliss.

As night descends with stars aglow,
Winter's wish begins to flow.
Wrapped in warmth, together we stand,
In the dance of snow, hand in hand.

A Breach in the Ice

The silence of winter, stark and still,
A crack in the ice, a void to fill.
Beneath the surface, secrets lay,
Whispering softly, come what may.

Nature holds breath, a moment's pause,
Witness of wonder, without a cause.
Fragments of sunlight dance on the hue,
A fragile world, painted anew.

Footsteps echo, breaking the trance,
In the chill, hope dares to dance.
Patterns of frost, delicate lace,
Each breath a story, time won't erase.

From the depths, the water sings,
A melody born of winter's wings.
In quiet corners, life still grows,
Amidst the beauty, the heart knows.

The breach in the ice, a sole refrain,
Shared between joy, and gentle pain.
Enduring moments, both harsh and sweet,
In winter's grasp, our spirits meet.

Solace of Shimmering Snow

Snowflakes descend, a silent grace,
Blanketing earth in a soft embrace.
Whispers of winter fill the air,
A sanctuary found, beyond compare.

Each flake a dream, unique and bright,
Sparkling diamonds under the light.
Drifting softly, the world transformed,
In shimmering silence, the heart is warmed.

Footprints wane, as shadows grow,
Wrapped in stillness, we seek the glow.
Trees wear white, like cloaks of peace,
In the beauty of snow, all worries cease.

The soft crunch beneath, a melody sweet,
In this tranquil moment, time feels complete.
Solace in silence, we pause and reflect,
Nature's embrace, a gentle connect.

As twilight falls, the scene aglow,
With every flake, our spirits flow.
In the solace found amidst the night,
Shimmering snow, our hearts take flight.

Veiled in Shards of Light

In the dawn's soft glow, we find,
Whispers of dreams, intertwined.
Each ray a story, softly told,
Awakening visions, bright and bold.

Shadows dance in the morning mist,
Moments of magic, too sweet to resist.
Fragments of hope, scattered around,
In each glimmer, our hearts are bound.

Time drips like dew from leaves,
Promising wonders that the heart believes.
With every sparkle, a path unrolled,
Guiding our spirits to visions untold.

Grounded in faith, we rise above,
Embracing the warmth of tender love.
Veiled in the colors of dreams so bright,
We journey onward, in shards of light.

Love's gentle tether and friendships shine,
In this radiant world, everything's fine.
Together we wander, side by side,
In the radiant dance where hopes abide.

Chilling Embrace of Aspirations

Within the frost of a starry night,
Dreams gather close, ready to take flight.
Each breath a whisper, cool and clear,
In the tranquil stillness, our goals appear.

Silent wishes float on the breeze,
Cultivating courage, aiming to please.
With every heartbeat, a story unfolds,
In the chilling air, our destiny holds.

Fingers trace paths of the unknown,
Guided by passions, brightly shown.
Embraced by shadows that whisper low,
Through icy realms, our spirits will grow.

Projecting visions that climb so high,
We learn to soar, to touch the sky.
In the depths of winter, warmth ignites,
As aspirations evaporate into nights.

Hand in hand, we chase the glow,
Through chilling moments, our passions flow.
United in purpose, we will embrace,
The chilling shadows, our dreams will chase.

Snowflakes of Silent Longing

Falling softly, the snowflakes drift,
Each one unique, like a secret gift.
They whisper tales of silent grace,
In winter's embrace, we find our place.

Frozen dreams in layers blend,
A tapestry woven that knows no end.
Every flake a hope, tender and small,
Gathering strength, we rise after the fall.

Under the moon's watchful eye,
The world lies still, as time slips by.
In this serene chill, hearts align,
Bound by a longing, pure and divine.

Echoes of warmth in the coldest nights,
Filling the silence with shimmering lights.
Through moments of stillness, we belong,
We dance together in nights so long.

In the blanket of white, memories weave,
Stories of longing we cherish and believe.
Together we wander, as time surely flows,
In the snowflakes of silent longing that glows.

Echoes of Resilience in Frost

In the clutches of winter's gale,
Resilience whispers, we will not fail.
With each frost, strength begins to rise,
Echoes of courage beneath the skies.

Hope clings to barren trees so stark,
In their silence, we find our spark.
Through chilling winds, we stand so tall,
Braving the storms, we will not fall.

Beneath the ice, the heart beats on,
Dreams intertwined, like dusk and dawn.
In every frosty breath, a tale
Of endurance, where spirits prevail.

With every step on frozen ground,
We forge ahead, where dreams abound.
In the dance of winter, we embrace the cost,
Finding our voices in echoes of frost.

Together we rise, as seasons shift,
In the heart of cold, we find our gift.
Echoes of resilience in every phase,
Guiding our way through winter's maze.

Hushed Anthems of the Cold

Whispers drift through frosted air,
Silent songs of winter's grace.
The world, a canvas dressed in white,
Peaceful dreams in soft embrace.

Brittle branches, silent cries,
Echoes fill the frozen night.
Stars are strangers in the skies,
Glistening with a muted light.

Distant mountains wrapped in haze,
Gently cloaked in icy guise.
Nature's breath in frosty phase,
Secrets dance where silence lies.

Footsteps crunch on glimmering ground,
Each sound sharp, yet bittersweet.
In this realm where wonders found,
Cold surrounds with tender heat.

Hushed anthems weave a tender bond,
In the stillness, spirits soar.
Through the chill, our hearts respond,
Embracing all that we adore.

Melodies of a Silent Frost

Crystalline whispers fill the air,
As frost weaves tunes on every tree.
Nature hums a gentle care,
Melodies of quiet glee.

Icicles hang like shimmering notes,
Tuning hearts to winter's song.
The world, lost in a soft hope,
Where the nights are warm and long.

Snowflakes twirl like dancers bright,
Spinning tales of pure delight.
In the hush, we find our way,
Guided by the moon's pale ray.

Every breath a frozen sigh,
Harmonies in the crystal breeze.
In this realm where echoes lie,
Beauty rests with tranquil ease.

Melodies of frost caress the night,
Wrapping dreams in icy sheets.
In this magic, all feels right,
As silence in the heart repeats.

In the Grip of Icebound Fantasies

Twilight dips in shades of blue,
A world stitched in glimmering frost.
In this realm, dreams feel anew,
Yet shadows linger, never lost.

Whispers cling to frozen trees,
Stories wrapped in chilly air.
Magic floats on winter's breeze,
An untouched realm, beyond compare.

Frozen rivers, quiet streams,
Reflecting wonders yet unseen.
In the grip of icy dreams,
Each moment feels like a serene.

Footsteps fade in soft disguise,
Lost within the silent score.
Underneath the starlit skies,
Hearts awaken to seek for more.

In the frost, we find our place,
Bound together through the chill.
In icebound dreams, we find grace,
And a warmth no frost can still.

Chasing Shadows in a Winter's Glare

In the snow, shadows dance and play,
Beneath the blue and white expanse.
Glistening trails will lead the way,
As winter calls for a soft romance.

Frosted fields stretch far and wide,
Whispering secrets to the hush.
Among the trees, the spirits glide,
Preparing for the evening rush.

Every step a whisper's grace,
Chasing dreams in the moon's stare.
In the quiet's warm embrace,
We discover love's pure glare.

Time slows down in winter's hold,
Where silence weaves its tender thread.
In the night, the stories told,
Of heartbeats shared, where shadows tread.

Through the chill, our spirits soar,
Chasing dreams in silent flight.
In the glow, we seek for more,
Wrapped in magic, endless night.

A Dream in the Deep Freeze

In shadows long, where silence sleeps,
Frozen whispers, the world it keeps.
Time dances slow, on ice it glides,
A dream unfolds, where hope abides.

In crystal halls, where visions play,
Stars twinkle bright, then drift away.
Frigid air holds secrets tight,
A swirling mist, both dark and light.

With every breath, a story breathes,
In winter's grip, the heart believes.
Softly brushed in frosty seams,
A canvas made of chilling dreams.

Yet in this cold, a fire burns,
For warmth is found in what one yearns.
So mid the ice, my spirit flies,
To seek the sun beyond the skies.

A deep freeze holds a fragile truth,
In silence, there is endless youth.
With every frost, I find my way,
In dreams alive, I long to stay.

Chilling Emotions

Underneath the winter's veil,
What lies hidden tells a tale.
Frigid breezes, hearts can ache,
In icy breath, old sorrows wake.

The snowflakes fall like tears of white,
Each one whispers, feels so right.
A chilling touch, a memory's call,
When warmth fades fast, we feel so small.

A shiver runs through silent lands,
Each heartbeat echoes, time like sands.
Frozen ponds reflect the night,
Chilling emotions, lost in flight.

Yet through the cold, the heart defies,
In frost's embrace, a fire flies.
From bitter winds, we find our song,
In chilling depths, we still belong.

So let the chill grip tight and fierce,
For in the dark, our hearts will pierce.
To warm the soul and breathe anew,
In chilling moments, love shines through.

Hibernate My Heart

When winter speaks in frosty tones,
I seek the warmth from ancient stones.
A quiet place to close my eyes,
To hibernate beneath the skies.

In layers thick, I tuck away,
The dreams that dance by light of day.
Snow blankets soft, a gentle shroud,
A silent space, away from crowd.

Beneath the ice, my heart will rest,
In frozen stillness, fears suppressed.
Time slows down in winter's grace,
A chance to pause, to find my place.

As storms may howl and winds may wail,
I find my peace, through winter's veil.
To rediscover who I am,
Hibernate my heart, I'll take a stand.

So let the world outside be cold,
Inside my shell, brave tales unfold.
When spring arrives, I will awake,
Rejoined with light, my path to take.

Worn Paths in Snow

The trail we take, where feet have tread,
Worn paths in snow, where stories spread.
Each step a trace of days gone by,
In frosted breath, the past will sigh.

Bound by memories, crisp and light,
Through swirling flakes, we chase the night.
These paths we carved, in white they gleam,
Echoes of laughter, faint like a dream.

With every turn, the chill remains,
Yet warmth ignites in hidden veins.
Worn paths in snow, a lover's lane,
Where footprints linger, love is gained.

Time leads us on, through drift and shade,
In snow's embrace, the heart's parade.
Worn paths in snow, a bond we make,
In frost's stillness, for love's sweet sake.

As seasons shift, so too will these,
Yet in their depths, my heart finds ease.
Together we roam, through winter's cheer,
Worn paths in snow, forever near.

Snowbound Stories

In silence deep, the winter breathes,
A world of white, where time deceives.
Footsteps soft on powdery ground,
Whispers of tales lost, yet found.

Branches heavy, draped in frost,
Every memory echoes, never lost.
Children laugh as snowflakes fall,
Nature's canvas, a serene call.

Around the fire, stories shared,
Warmth of hearts, none unprepared.
Each glowing ember holds a dream,
In nights of frost, where spirits gleam.

The moonlit sky, a shimmering show,
Guiding paths where soft winds blow.
In snowbound nights, our hearts align,
Crafting stories, yours and mine.

As dawn breaks clear, the magic fades,
Yet in our hearts, the joy cascades.
For winter's tale, forever spun,
In every heartbeat, the stories run.

A Whisper Beneath the Snow

Beneath the hush, the secrets sigh,
Where whispers linger as dreams fly.
Snowflakes dance on the quiet breeze,
Nature holds its breath with ease.

A frosty veil, the world a blur,
In this cocoon, the heart will stir.
Memories drift, soft as a sigh,
Under the stars, we wonder why.

In the chill, the warmth finds way,
Voices echo in shades of gray.
Each crystal flake, a tale unfolds,
Carried through the nights so cold.

Echoes of love in the stillness ring,
A gentle touch that winter brings.
Hope rests lightly on frozen ground,
In every whisper, peace is found.

The morning sun breaks through the mist,
A promise made, a timeless twist.
With open hearts, we dream anew,
Beneath the snow, the world feels true.

Dreams as White as Winter

Dreams take flight on wings of white,
Under the stars, in quiet night.
Softly they drift, like flakes that fall,
Embracing silence, a soothing call.

In the stillness, visions grow,
Every heartbeat starts to flow.
Warmed by thoughts of times gone by,
In winter's grasp, we learn to fly.

A blanket of snow, pure and bright,
Wrapping the world in gentle light.
Echoes of laughter, memories chase,
In frosty dreams, they find their place.

From dawn till dusk, the beauty stays,
In crisp white realms, we weave our ways.
Each whispered wish, a journey seen,
Through snowy fields, where hope has been.

With every breath, the silence swells,
In winter's heart, our story dwells.
Forever anchored, in dreams we trust,
As white as winter, pure and just.

Frosty Illusions

In the twilight, shadows play,
Frosty whispers lead astray.
Mirrored sparks on frozen streams,
Reflecting all our hidden dreams.

A world of wonder, trapped in ice,
Moments captured, never twice.
Every flake, a fleeting glance,
In frosty realms where spirits dance.

Hazy visions fade in light,
Crafting illusions, soft and slight.
Through the veil of winter's breath,
We find the beauty, even in death.

Yet in this magic, truth remains,
Underneath the cold, love reigns.
Each frosty breath, a secret shared,
In winter's heart, we are all bared.

As seasons shift, the truth breaks free,
From frosty illusions, we learn to see.
In every moment, hold it tight,
For winter's spell is pure delight.

Slumbering Under Snow

Soft flakes fall, blankets white,
Nature rests in calm delight.
Whispers of the winter night,
Dreams are kept till morning light.

Branches bow with frosty glow,
Hidden life beneath the snow.
Silent secrets, still and slow,
Await the sun, the springtime's show.

Footprints linger, then erased,
Time moves on, it won't be faced.
Snowflakes dance, a gentle taste,
Of winter's love, so sweetly laced.

Crisp air holds a breathless sigh,
Stars twinkle in the velvet sky.
Snowmen stand with eyes awry,
In a world where dreams can fly.

Underneath this frosty quilt,
Seeds of hope are gently built.
Spring will come, and hearts will tilt,
To greet the warmth that winter spilt.

Hibernation of Hope

In the shadows, dreams reside,
Wrapped in warmth, where fears subside.
Nature's pause, a gentle glide,
Hope lies waiting, deep inside.

Stars above a frozen lake,
Whispers stir, as night will wake.
Silent vows that hearts can make,
In the cold, like threads we stake.

Crystals form on window frames,
Every breath, a puff of flames.
Hibernation, sweet refrains,
Life's rhythms, gently claims.

Days grow short, the sun's retreat,
Nature sleeps, and stillness greets.
Yet in quiet, softly beats,
The pulse of spring in snowy sheets.

Awake, arise, as light draws near,
Hope unfurls, dispelling fear.
Winter's grip cannot steer,
Life returns, the skies will clear.

Winter's Silken Lullaby

Silk of snow on whispered ground,
A lullaby without a sound.
Cuddled in its cool surround,
Nature's heart beats safe and sound.

Hushed are streets, as shadows blend,
Time slows down, as seasons mend.
In winter's grasp, we comprehend,
Moments shared, we cannot pretend.

Breath of twilight paints the scene,
Frosted branches glimmering sheen.
Every whisper, soft and clean,
Winter holds you in between.

Frozen lakes in silver light,
Stars above, a pure delight.
Wrapped in dusk, we hold on tight,
To dreams that dance through endless night.

As snowflakes drop in silent prayer,
Hope will rise, so light and fair.
In sweet slumber, we will care,
For spring's warm kiss is waiting there.

Frigid Enchantment

A crystal land, where magic glows,
Frigid air with frosty prose.
Every flake, an art that flows,
Charmed beneath the moonlight's shows.

Whispers echo through the trees,
In the silence, feel the breeze.
Winter's spell, a gentle tease,
Carving dreams with perfect ease.

Icicles promise bright refrains,
Beauty drapes on window panes.
In the chill, the heart contains,
Memories like snow, a chains.

Step by step, a world anew,
Every moment feels like dew.
Watch the stars, a cosmic cue,
As hope ignites with each view.

Frigid nights bring warmth to hold,
Secrets of the winter told.
Through the cold, we all are bold,
In the heart, the fire unfolds.

Beneath a Blanket of Ice

Silent whispers in the night,
Stars twinkle with frosty light.
Nature sleeps in still repose,
Wrapped in warmth, the cold wind blows.

Branches heavy, laden with white,
A world transformed, pure and bright.
Footprints crunch on glistening ground,
In this hush, magic is found.

Frozen rivers, gentle flow,
Carving paths in sheets of snow.
A crystal realm, serene and bright,
Beneath a blanket, cloaked in white.

The moon casts shadows, soft and wide,
As dreams of warmth within reside.
In the chill, warmth we seek,
Beneath the ice, hope won't be weak.

Nature's breath, a frozen sigh,
In quiet moments, we rely.
Beneath the ice, the heart beats slow,
In winter's grasp, love will grow.

Muffled Beats in Winter's Grasp

Snowflakes dance on whispered winds,
 Muffled beats where silence begins.
 A world asleep, wrapped in dreams,
 Where every shadow softly gleams.

Icicles hang like crystal spears,
 Guarding secrets, holding fears.
The crisp air bites, yet hearts are warm,
 In winter's grasp, we find our calm.

Fires crackle in twilight's glow,
 Stories shared as embers flow.
Outside, the landscape wears its crown,
 Of white, serene, and softly brown.

With each breath, the world stands still,
 Wrapped in peace, the soul we fill.
 Underneath the starlit sky,
 In winter's grasp, our dreams can fly.

As dawn breaks, painting skies anew,
 With hues of pink and icy blue.
 Muffled beats, a heart's refrain,
 Echo softly through the gain.

A Cascade of Frosted Fantasies

In the twilight where shadows weave,
Dreams emerge that we believe.
A cascade of frost, pure delight,
In every flake, a wish takes flight.

Pines adorned in soft embrace,
Nature's canvas, a wintry grace.
Whispers linger on the breeze,
In every moment, hearts find ease.

Glistening fields stretch far and wide,
Where laughter echoes, joy can't hide.
Children play in the drifts of snow,
Creating memories that brightly glow.

Underneath the silvered moon,
A world harmonizes to winter's tune.
As dreams cascade in frosted streams,
Life seems woven from our dreams.

Through the cold, warmth sparks ignite,
Binding us close through the night.
In every heartbeat, fantasies swell,
A cascade of stories, we tell.

Winter's Embrace, Silent and Deep

In silent woods where shadows creep,
Winter's embrace, tranquil and deep.
Blankets of snow on every bough,
In this stillness, we take a vow.

Breath of frost on air so clear,
Each exhale captures moments near.
Footfalls soft on frozen ground,
In winter's arms, peace is found.

A fir tree stands, adorned in white,
Guardian of dreams in the night.
With every breeze, a shivering chill,
Yet hearts grow warm, reflecting will.

In the stillness, time slows its pace,
Fleeting thoughts in winter's grace.
Silent whispers through the trees,
Winter's embrace, a soft release.

Against the cold, our spirits rise,
Finding warmth in tender ties.
In every heartbeat, love's decree,
Winter's embrace, silent and free.

Icy Echoes of the Heart

In winter's grasp, the silence sings,
Whispers dance on frostbitten wings.
A crystal tear falls from the sky,
Memories linger, they never die.

Footsteps fade on the powdered ground,
Echoes of love in spaces abound.
Frozen dreams wrapped in soft white,
Haunting shadows embrace the night.

The heart beats slow beneath the cold,
Stories woven in threads of gold.
Through icy veins, warmth tries to flow,
Yet bittersweet is the love we know.

Chill winds carry what once was near,
A heart's lament, both sweet and clear.
In frozen time, we search for signs,
Of passion's flame, in sacred lines.

With every breath, the stillness grows,
Life's bitter-sweetness gently flows.
In icy echoes, we find our way,
Through winter's heart, we dare to stay.

Ethereal Frost on Sleep's Edge

In twilight's glow, the world alights,
Softly draped in frosty whites.
Stars twinkle like a lover's gaze,
Ethereal dreams in a shimmering haze.

The silence wraps the whispered night,
Holding secrets, pure and bright.
Snowflakes fall like whispered prayers,
Cocooned in peace, free of cares.

A gentle hush upon the land,
Winter's touch, a tender hand.
As eyelids fall, the spirit soars,
Cradled in the warmth that endures.

In slumber deep, the heart will freeze,
Held captive by the gentle breeze.
Yet in the stillness, life's pulse flows,
Awakening in the frost that glows.

Ethereal frost, a soft embrace,
Guiding dreams to a sacred place.
Each breath a sigh, in chilled delight,
On sleep's edge, we dance with night.

A Snowy Lullaby

Snowflakes whirl in a magical dance,
Cradling dreams in a wintry trance.
Each flake a whisper, soft and light,
Gently falling to kiss the night.

The world transforms, a canvas pure,
Blanketed secrets, soft and sure.
A lullaby sung by the softest breeze,
Wrapping the heart in soothing ease.

Trees stand tall in coats of white,
Guardians of secrets held tight.
In this hush, the soul finds rest,
Wrapped in calm, the heart is blessed.

A child's laughter, a joy so bright,
Echoes through the frosty night.
Creating memories in the snow,
A snowy lullaby, soft and slow.

As dreams take flight on winter's breath,
Life whispers softly, defying death.
In snowy realms, our spirits fly,
Comfort finds us, a sweet lullaby.

Suspended Moments in Chill

Time stands still in this frosty air,
Suspended moments, beyond compare.
The world breathes deep, cloaked in white,
As Echoes linger through the night.

Shadows cast by a pale moonlight,
Reveal the beauty of the night.
Branches bare hold treasures divine,
In quietude, our souls entwine.

Each heartbeat feels the winter's sting,
As snowflakes fall, the echoes sing.
Suspended in moments, lost in thought,
The chill embraces what winter brought.

We gather warmth in stories told,
In frosty breaths, find courage bold.
Drifting dreams like white kites soar,
Suspended in chill, we yearn for more.

In silent awe, we find our way,
Through frozen sparks of yesterday.
Each moment cherished, deeply felt,
In winter's grasp, our hearts will melt.

The Crystal Veil of Desires Untold

In shadows deep, where wishes crawl,
A crystal veil, so thin, so tall.
Behind its sheen, all dreams reside,
In whispers soft, they yearn to glide.

Glimmers twinkling, secrets bright,
Each hope a spark, igniting night.
In silence thick, they softly weave,
A tapestry of what we believe.

Yet paths remain, so seldom trod,
In pursuit of love, we seek the nod.
With hearts aflame and spirits bold,
We chase the tales that life has told.

As breathless moments drift away,
Desires dance, and fears decay.
The crystal veil, our guide divine,
In its embrace, our souls align.

Through myriad veils, we stitch and sew,
A fabric rich, from joy to woe.
With every thread, a story spun,
Desires bloom; the dance's begun.

Enchanted by a Frost-Gilded Veil

Moonlit nights with frost adorned,
The world in white, a dream reborn.
A gilded veil, the chill, the grace,
In frozen whispers, time finds place.

Each snowflake sparkles, pure and bright,
A shimmer caught in silver light.
With every breath, we chase the thrill,
In icy realms, our hearts instill.

Beneath the veil, enchantment flows,
Where silent magic gently grows.
Our laughter dances on the breeze,
With every glance, the heart agrees.

In winter's arms, we find our song,
An echo sweet, where we belong.
Through frosted paths, we wander far,
United still, beneath the star.

Yet shadows linger, veiled in ice,
As we embrace the cold's entice.
With every step, the journey calls,
In frost-gilded dreams, our spirit sprawls.

Ember Dreams on an Icy Frontier

On icy plains where silence reigns,
Ember dreams flicker, break the chains.
In every spark, a fiery glow,
Awakening hope in winter's foe.

The frontier stretches, vast and bright,
While shadows curl, engulf the light.
Yet still we dance, with hearts ablaze,
Embracing warmth in icy haze.

Through frozen fields, where whispers dwell,
The ember's glow casts a warm spell.
Each step ignites a tale untold,
Of dreams reborn and hearts so bold.

In nature's hush, our spirits soar,
While icy winds beg for more.
With ember dreams to guide our flight,
We forge ahead through deepest night.

So let us chase the warmth within,
With every spark, a chance to win.
On this frontier, where hope ignites,
We'll find our way through endless nights.

Hopes Suspended in a Shimmering Freeze

In winter's breath, our hopes reside,
Suspended still, like stars that guide.
A shimmering freeze, a realm so bright,
Where dreams embrace the longest night.

Each glimmer tells of wishes cast,
A gentle touch of seasons past.
With open hearts, we seek the glow,
In frozen realms, love's whispers flow.

The crystal air, a canvas wide,
Holds stories bright in silence bide.
Each frozen sigh, a vow so true,
In this embrace, we become anew.

Through nights adorned with silver lace,
We find our strength in nature's grace.
While hopes suspended, silent freeze,
Awaken now, beneath the trees.

So let us wander, hand in hand,
Embracing dreams that understand.
In shimmering folds, our spirits freeze,
While hopes ignite like winter's breeze.

Shards of a Winter's Wish

In the stillness of the night,
Whispers of frost take flight.
Dreams woven in silver light,
Shattered hopes within our sight.

A longing that curls with the breeze,
Frigid echoes through the trees.
Each moment freezes, never to cease,
In the heart, a fragile peace.

Glimmers held in icy shards,
Guarded truths behind the guards.
With every breath, the world regards,
Winter's wish in silent cards.

Time drifts slowly, cold and pure,
Embers of warmth we can't procure.
Yet in the midst of frost, we're sure,
Every shard we hold endures.

As dawn approaches, shadows fade,
Hope emerges from the cascade.
With every step, new paths are laid,
Winter's wish, a serenade.

Frigid Visions at Dusk

At dusk, the world turns pale,
Candles flicker, ghosts prevail.
Through the silence, whispers sail,
Frigid visions weave their tale.

A breath of chill in twilight's grasp,
Stars awaken, ready to clasp.
Hopes arise, like shadows rasp,
In the dark, we find our gasp.

The moon, a beacon in the night,
Guides the way with silver light.
Each step forward feels so right,
In frigid visions, hearts take flight.

With winter's cloak, we wander far,
Tracing dreams beneath each star.
In quiet moments, we spar,
Frigid visions, never bizarre.

As day yields to the starry dome,
We chase the night, forever roam.
With every heartbeat, find our home,
In frigid visions, we are known.

Silent Shimmer of Ambition

In the silence, dreams take wing,
Softly, like the cold winds sing.
Ambition's glow, a subtle thing,
Shimmers bright in every spring.

A whisper speaks of paths untrod,
Through the shadows where we plod.
Each step forward, a silent nod,
In ambition's heart, no fraud.

Mountains loom, yet we embrace,
The quiet strength we interlace.
With every trial, we find our pace,
Silent shimmer, a steadfast grace.

Though doubts may rise, we stand aligned,
With visions clear, our fates entwined.
In the stillness, bliss defined,
Silent shimmer, love refined.

Beyond horizons, futures gleam,
Ambition whispers, fuels our dream.
There's power in our shared esteem,
Silent shimmer, we redeem.

Crystalized Yearnings

Yearnings hang like frosted breath,
In the stillness, shadows dress.
Crystalized in ice, not death,
Hope transforms with each caress.

With every glisten, dreams unfold,
Stories spun, while hearts are bold.
Winter's kiss, both fierce and cold,
Crystalized yearnings, tales retold.

In every flake, a promise lies,
Underneath the leaden skies.
With whispers soft, they start to rise,
Yearnings breathe where silence cries.

The world transforms in shades of white,
Echoes linger, soft delight.
In crystal dreams, we seek the light,
Yearnings forged in winter's night.

Yet as seasons shift and bend,
Yearnings mold, they do not end.
In every heart, new passions blend,
Crystalized, our spirits send.

White Veils of Longing

In the mist, I see your face,
Whispers soft in a quiet space.
Veils of yearning, soft and white,
Drawing me into the night.

Moonlit shadows dance and play,
Calling memories that fade away.
Through the haze, I search for you,
A love that always feels so true.

Time may pass like fleeting dreams,
Yet your essence forever gleams.
In the silence, hearts entwine,
Lost in thoughts, where we align.

Every echo, a tender sigh,
In the darkness, we still fly.
Threads of hope woven tight,
In white veils, we find our light.

Shivers from Silent Nights

Winter's breath, a soft caress,
Whispers chill, yet still impress.
Stars peek through the darkened skies,
Silent nights with hidden cries.

Canvas blank, the world asleep,
Into shadows, secrets creep.
Frosted whispers in the air,
Shivers dance without a care.

Footprints trace the path I tread,
Every moment, softly said.
In the stillness, hearts can soar,
Silent nights, we long for more.

Breath of winter, softly sighs,
Wonders hide beneath cold skies.
In the quiet, dreams ignite,
Shivers felt in silent night.

Ghosts in the Frost

Frosty mornings, eerily bright,
Whispers linger, ghosts in flight.
Shadows echoed in the trees,
Stories carried by the breeze.

Memories rise in silver sheen,
Figures fade, but still they gleam.
Every breath a chilling spell,
In the frost where echoes dwell.

Footsteps haunt the frozen ground,
Silent voices all around.
In the twilight, shadows blend,
Ghostly presences that won't end.

Nature's canvas, cold and bare,
Whispers feel like ghostly prayer.
Within the frost, they dance and sway,
Lost in time, they find their way.

Dreams Drift in the Freeze

In the stillness, dreams take flight,
Float like snowflakes in the night.
Crisp and clear, a world anew,
Chasing hopes that feel so true.

Time suspended, moments freeze,
Glimmers spark with gentle ease.
Every heart a drifting tale,
Across the winter's silver veil.

Stars reflect on icy streams,
Carrying whispers of our dreams.
In the warmth, we softly glow,
Through the freeze, our spirits flow.

Wrapped in blankets, snug and tight,
We embrace the winter's bite.
Dreams will rise with morning's light,
Drifting on through endless night.

Icy Glistens of Forgotten Dreams

In whispers of the night, they fade,
Lost echoes of a promise made.
Shadows dance on frozen streams,
Caught in icy glistens of forgotten dreams.

What once was bright now shimmers cold,
Stories left silently told.
A blanket of frost on hopes once bright,
In the stillness of a frosty night.

The moon hangs low, a silver sigh,
Reflecting tears that dare not dry.
Each twinkle speaks of wishes past,
A fleeting moment, fading fast.

Beneath the frost, the heartbeat's sound,
An ember of warmth is still found.
In the quiet, dreams softly weep,
In icy glistens, memories sleep.

Yet as dawn breaks with golden hue,
A promise whispers, brave and true.
For even in cold, the heart can gleam,
Awakening from forgotten dreams.

Frosting the Strings of Desire

A melody drifts through winter air,
Notes like whispers, tender and rare.
Frosting the strings with delicate grace,
Each sound ensnares, a warm embrace.

Through shivering branches, the music flows,
Woven with secrets, a tale that grows.
Crystalline accents, sweetened and pure,
Binding our hearts, a soft allure.

As twilight descends, the sky holds tight,
Stars touch the earth with a spark of light.
In shadows deep, the notes entwine,
Frosting the strings of desires benign.

With every chord, a promise is spun,
Of dreams united, two hearts as one.
The air is thick with longing's tune,
Beneath the watchful, silver moon.

So let the frost on our passions play,
In this winter night, we'll find our way.
For even cold can warm the soul,
Frosting the strings that make us whole.

A Charmed Moment in Hibernation

Wrapped in stillness, time stands still,
Nature whispers, a gentle thrill.
In the hush of sleep, dreams softly glide,
A charmed moment, where hearts reside.

Snowflakes drift, a silent song,
Cradling dreams as they float along.
The world outside, blanketed and white,
While warmth surrounds in cozy light.

Each breath is soft, a rhythm slow,
In this haven, love starts to grow.
Underneath the layers, sparks ignite,
A charmed moment, pure and bright.

As shadows dance and daylight fades,
Time holds still in its warm cascades.
In this embrace, the heart's delight,
A charmed moment in hibernation's night.

Spring will come with a vibrant call,
But for now, in silence, we stand tall.
In the calm of the cold, spirits soar,
A charmed moment to cherish and adore.

Shivering Hope in the Silence

In the quiet spaces, hope takes flight,
Whispers of warmth in the depth of night.
Shivering softly, the heart finds its way,
In the silence, dreams gently sway.

Snow on the branches, a heavy dress,
Each flake a promise, each pause, a guess.
A flicker of light in the darkest hour,
Shivering hope holds a hidden power.

Beneath the surface, life stirs alive,
In dormant dreams, the spirit will thrive.
The stillness embraces, a tender touch,
Shivering hopes that mean so much.

As stars keep watch in the endless sky,
In the silence, we learn to fly.
For even in cold, there's warmth to find,
Shivering hope, a love so blind.

When spring awakens with colors bold,
The echoes of winter will turn to gold.
Yet in the silence, our hearts will know,
Shivering hope is where we grow.

The Hushed Palette of Winter

Frosted branches dance in light,
Soft whispers weave through the night.
A canvas draped in silver hues,
Nature's breath in tranquil views.

Icicles hang like crystal dreams,
Silent echoes fill the streams.
Shadows stretch with evening's glow,
In this stillness, time feels slow.

Footprints pressed in powdered white,
Hushed secrets held, pure delight.
Every flake a silent tale,
In winter's breath, we softly sail.

The world adorned in pale embrace,
Silent wonders fill the space.
A palette drawn by nature's hand,
In winter's grip, our hearts shall stand.

Beneath the moon's soft, glowing beam,
Life pauses for a fleeting dream.
In the hush, our hopes take flight,
Wrapped in winter's tender night.

Cold Currents of Memory

Winds that wander through the trees,
Carry whispers on the breeze.
Frozen echoes of the past,
Moments captured, meant to last.

Each heartbeat in the biting air,
Sparks of warmth, a tender care.
Frigid thoughts in layers deep,
In twilight's arms, the shadows creep.

Ghostly laughter, soft and clear,
Dances lightly, holds us near.
Memories wrapped in winter's shroud,
Cloaked in silence, soft and loud.

Time's embrace, a chilling grip,
Fleeting visions in a slip.
Cold currents flow with every breath,
In the frost, we find our depth.

As stars peer through the velvet night,
Old stories weave their fragile light.
Through the chill, the heart stays warm,
In cold currents, we find our calm.

Crystal Frost on Silent Nights

A quiet world, draped in white,
Crystal frost on silent nights.
Each breath hangs in the crisp air,
Magic twinkles everywhere.

Stars reflect on icy lakes,
As nature stirs, and gently wakes.
Underneath the moon's soft glow,
Frosty dreams begin to flow.

Snowflakes fall like whispered dreams,
Veiling earth in shimmery seams.
Presence felt in every flake,
Awakening what's held awake.

Blades of grass in frozen glades,
Painted with the night's parades.
In the hush, the heart finds peace,
Silent moments that never cease.

Through the night, the world stands still,
In quiet awe, we drink our fill.
Crystal frost on every breath,
Celebrating winter's depth.

Snowflakes of Unfulfilled Wishes

Falling gently from the skies,
Snowflakes whisper soft goodbyes.
Each one holds a dream so bright,
Unfulfilled beneath the night.

Wishes made in secret tones,
Carried far on chilly moans.
The wind will sing what hearts conceal,
As frozen tears begin to heal.

In each flake, a story told,
Of hope, of love, of hearts of gold.
Yet as they touch the earth below,
We must wait for what we sow.

With every flake, there's bittersweet,
A longing shared, a cosmic feat.
In winter's grasp, our dreams will dance,
In swirling snow, a fleeting chance.

Yet through the chill, we hold our fire,
Dreams remain, they never tire.
In snowflakes, wishes drift and flow,
Waiting for spring's tender glow.

Wraiths of Ice on Slumbering Shores

Wraiths of ice dance in the night,
Casting shadows, pure and white.
Upon the shores, the silence stays,
Wrapped in frost, a world that plays.

Moonlight glimmers on the sea,
Whispers carried, wild and free.
In the stillness, secrets flow,
As the currents ebb and glow.

Frozen tides of deep despair,
Search for warmth in frosty air.
Yet the stars, they keep their watch,
Guiding dreams, a silent touch.

Footprints vanish on the sand,
Gone like hopes, like dreams unplanned.
In this realm of crystal chill,
Nature's canvas, stark yet still.

Echoes linger, soft and pale,
In the night, a haunting tale.
Wraiths of ice on slumbering shores,
Guard the peace that nature pours.

Eclipsed by a Frosted Dream

In the twilight, shadows blend,
Winter's breath begins to mend.
Silent worlds in frost are spun,
Eclipsed by dreams, the night has begun.

Stars like diamonds, shyly gleam,
Wrapped in a cold, enchanting dream.
The moon hides behind clouds of gray,
As night unfolds, bright thoughts decay.

Crimson dawn on frosted hills,
Awakens hearts, yet silence chills.
Time stands still in icy grace,
Where whispers linger, lost in space.

Through frozen branches, echoes sigh,
Beneath the weight of endless sky.
In the hush, our thoughts may roam,
Eclipsed by dreams, we drift from home.

Fragments of warmth, like grains of sand,
Fleeting moments we cannot withstand.
In this cold, vast, timeless stream,
We find our solace, a frosted dream.

The Chilling Breath of Whispers

The chilling breath of whispers near,
Creeps through shadows, crystal clear.
In the night, where secrets hide,
Echoes dance, with ghosts as guide.

Frozen winds weave stories told,
Of ancient times, of hearts so bold.
Underneath the silent snow,
A haunting melody flows slow.

Branches crack, the moonlight fades,
Casting spells in frosted glades.
In the dark, the spirits stir,
Painting dreams that softly blur.

Whispers of the stars align,
Mingling thoughts in tangled vine.
In this realm of icy breath,
Life and death, a dance of wealth.

Listen close to what they share,
If you dare to breathe the air.
Through the chill, our hearts may find,
The chilling breath, a thread entwined.

Marooned in a Crystal Landscape

Marooned in a crystal land,
Where frost and silence go hand in hand.
Glistening trees like diamonds bright,
Hold their breath in the still of night.

Endless fields of sparkling white,
Stretch beneath the moon's soft light.
In this world, our worries freeze,
Carried away on winter's breeze.

Each footstep crunches, crisp and clear,
Echoing dreams we hold so dear.
Time drifts on like trailing snow,
As the frosty winds gently blow.

Landscapes shift, a painter's brush,
Creates a scene that makes us hush.
Lost in beauty, hearts align,
Marooned in dreams, pure and divine.

Beneath the stars, we stand as one,
Under the glow of a distant sun.
In this realm, our spirits soar,
Marooned in a land we adore.

Beneath the Surface of Frost

Under quiet whispers of the night,
Silent secrets frozen tight,
Beneath the layers, life still breathes,
Hope awakens as winter weaves.

Crystals glisten on the ground,
In the silence, peace is found,
Branches shiver, withhold their dreams,
Nature stirs in silver gleams.

Footprints mark the frosty hue,
Leading paths to skies so blue,
In the stillness, hearts convene,
Beneath the frost, love is seen.

Hidden warmth in every freeze,
Softened heart, like gentle breeze,
Life awaits in waiting grace,
Beneath the frost, we find our place.

When sun descends, and night takes hold,
Stories whispered, tales retold,
In the frost, a world of dreams,
A canvas bright with silver beams.

Dreams Caught in a Winter's Tale

In the hush of winter's breath,
Whispers dance, life and death,
Softly falling, snowflakes veil,
Woven deep in every tale.

Fires flicker, shadows play,
Drawing night from fading day,
Underneath the blanket's glow,
Dreams entwined, like falling snow.

Time stands still in evening's hue,
Moments captured, pure and true,
Chasing visions, hearts ablaze,
In the hush of chilly days.

With each flake that finds its way,
Stories gather, hopes display,
In the winter's chilly grasp,
Dreams are held in warmth's sweet clasp.

Through the veil of frosty light,
Every wish takes permanent flight,
In this realm of white and grey,
Dreams are caught, they softly sway.

Flickering Flames in Crystal Caress

In the hearth, embers softly glow,
Against the chill, they dance and flow,
Flickering shadows, whispers near,
In crystal caress, warmth draws near.

Wrapped in blankets, hearts ignited,
Moments cherished, love delighted,
Every spark, a story told,
In the night, bright flames unfold.

Through the window, frost designs,
Patterns woven, nature shines,
In every flame, reflections fade,
Memories in the twilight made.

With every crackle, dreams ascend,
In the warmth, our souls transcend,
Outside, winter's chill may bite,
But here we hold the heart's pure light.

And as the night surrounds us tight,
In flickering flames, we find our sight,
In crystal caress, the world sleeps,
Together, forever, our love keeps.

The Wintery Haze of Desire

When twilight falls in frosty haze,
Desire dances in whispered praise,
Every glance, a spark ignites,
In the winter, passion lights.

Snowflakes drift, a yearning sigh,
Wrapped in dreams, we wander by,
Breath condenses, hearts align,
In the stillness, bodies intertwine.

Through the maze of twinkling stars,
Time stands still, erasing scars,
In tender moments, warmth ignites,
We breathe together through the nights.

Every heartbeat, every touch,
In winter's grip, we crave so much,
The world may freeze in quiet air,
But in our hearts, we boldly dare.

In fleeting seconds, love's embrace,
Under winter's softest lace,
Bound by dreams, we twirl and sway,
In the haze, we find our way.

A Glacial Portrait of Night

In the stillness, shadows creep,
Beneath the moon's soft, silver sweep.
Stars like diamonds, cold and bright,
Whisper secrets deep in the night.

Frosted whispers kiss the ground,
Echoing dreams that swirl around.
Each breath visible, a ghostly trail,
Lost in wonders, where spirits sail.

Trees stand solemn, dressed in white,
Branches tangled, a silent sight.
Every flake a work of art,
Crafted gently, a frozen heart.

Time stands still, as if to pause,
Nature's breath holds, just because.
In this portrait, calm and clear,
The night unfolds, serene and near.

As dawn approaches, hues ignite,
Fleeting warmth in morning light.
Yet in twilight, as shadows blend,
A glacial night will not soon end.

In the Realm of Frostbitten Enchantment

Across the land, a magic spell,
Frostbitten tales begin to swell.
Each branch adorned with icy lace,
Nature's cloak, a cold embrace.

Whispers dance upon the breeze,
Frost invokes a chill with ease.
Crystals sparkle, reflecting dreams,
In this realm, nothing as it seems.

Time slows down beneath the stars,
Spirits wander, near and far.
Every glimmer, a hidden wish,
In frozen air, our voices swish.

Night deepens, shadows play,
In this realm, night meets day.
Footsteps trail where few have sought,
In frostbitten wonders, we are caught.

As morning breaks, enchantment wanes,
Yet in silence, magic reigns.
For in winter's cold embrace,
Each heart carries this sacred space.

Imprints of Dreams on Chilled Canvas

Underneath a blanket white,
Dreams emerge with the first light.
Each footprint tells a hidden tale,
Across the canvas, soft and pale.

Snowflakes dance like thoughts set free,
In this stillness, we can see.
Shapes and shadows start to form,
A fleeting moment, nature's charm.

Winter's breath, an artist's stroke,
Chilled whispers turn to ghostly cloak.
Imprints linger, then they fade,
As warmth returns, the silence made.

The horizon blushes, night retreats,
Chilled canvas holds our heartbeats.
Each fleeting moment holds a spark,
In dreams that wander, gentle and stark.

Yet in memory, they remain,
Imprinted dreams that hold no chain.
In a world of frost and grace,
We find our peace in winter's face.

The Stillness of Winter's Embrace

A hush descends across the land,
Winter wraps us, gentle hand.
Cold caresses, soft as night,
In stillness found, a pure delight.

Silvery moons reflect and glow,
Casting shadows, deep and slow.
Every flake falls with a sigh,
Embraced by silence, we comply.

Branches bow with heavy grace,
Winter whispers, time and space.
Echoes linger, frosty air,
In this stillness, hearts laid bare.

Days grow short, and nights are long,
Yet in cold, we find our song.
The warmth within, a fire bright,
Brightening the chill of night.

As seasons shift and time moves on,
The stillness whispers, dusk to dawn.
In winter's hold, we find our place,
In the embrace of nature's grace.

Dreamscapes of the Shivering Sky

A canvas of blue, so vast and wide,
Clouds drift lazily, with secrets to hide.
Sunlight dances on edges, so bright,
While shadows whisper of the approaching night.

In the hush of dawn, dreams take their flight,
Softly they glimmer, a magical sight.
The horizon beckons, horizons anew,
Painting the sky with every hue.

Stars twinkle softly, like eyes from afar,
Guiding the dreamers, wherever they are.
Each breath of the night, a promise to keep,
Awakening visions, borne from deep sleep.

With each fleeting moment, the dreams intertwine,
In the expanse above, where the worlds align.
Echoes of laughter, in whispers they play,
As night swallows daylight, and night turns to day.

So wander the valleys of shimmering skies,
With hearts as our compass, and hope as our prize.
In dreamscapes untouched, we seek to explore,
For the shivering sky holds so much more.

Silent Echoes on Winter's Path

In the blanket of white, where silence lays deep,
Winter whispers softly, secrets to keep.
Footsteps crunch gently on a frostbitten trail,
As shadows grow longer, and daylight grows pale.

Hushed are the woods, in their icy embrace,
Nature wears stillness, a tranquil face.
Barren branches stretch, reaching for skies,
Carrying echoes of long-lost goodbyes.

The breath of the cold, a ghostly refrain,
Calls to the heart, with a bittersweet pain.
Each flake that descends, a story untold,
Dancing through twilight, both fragile and bold.

Moonlight spills silver, on the frost-kissed ground,
In this winter's dream, lost souls are found.
The chill wraps around like an old, worn quilt,
Binding our thoughts to everything built.

So walk through the silence, embrace the cold,
For winter's soft echoes, are treasures to hold.
In the heart of the winter, where dreams softly fade,
Awaits a new journey, where memories are made.

The Color of Cold Whispers

In twilight's embrace, where shadows converge,
Cold whispers beckon, as if to emerge.
A palette of silence, brushed with the night,
Each hue a reflection, of dreams taking flight.

Pale blues and greys, paint the canvas so fine,
Echoes of winter in every line.
Beneath the soft stars, the world holds its breath,
For the color of cold speaks of life and of death.

Whispers of warmth in the chill of the air,
Flicker like fireflies, elusive and rare.
Moments suspended, in delicate frost,
Together we wander, what may be lost.

The color of cold weaves a tale in the dawn,
As night surrenders, and dreams slowly yawn.
In shades of remembrance, we find our way,
Through the whispers of night, into the day.

So listen to nature's soft, haunting song,
In colors of cold, where the heart feels strong.
For even in winter, the whispers won't die,
In the warmth of each heartbeat, they continue to fly.

Imprisoned Wishes of Winter

Beneath the frost, where the shadows abide,
Imprisoned wishes in winter reside.
With every snowflake that falls from above,
Dreams slip like whispers, wrapped in cold love.

They linger in silence, like echoes unheard,
Waiting for moments, like soft, spoken word.
Each wish a glimmer, a flicker of light,
Trapped in the stillness, hidden from sight.

Through frosted windows, we peer into night,
Hoping for warmth in the absence of light.
The chill of the air clings close like a friend,
A reminder of promises that may never end.

So gather your hopes, and let them take flight,
Turn imprisoned wishes into pure insight.
For even in winter, when the world seems asleep,
The heart holds its dreams, so precious to keep.

In the stillness of snow, find the beauty within,
Of wishes unfurling, like paper-thin skin.
With each breath of cold, let your spirit soar free,
For the winter may bind, but it also sets free.

Whispers of the Icy Moon

In the night, a hush unfolds,
Silver beams on tales untold.
Shadows dance in silent grace,
Underneath the moon's embrace.

Frosted whispers weave their thread,
In the light, secrets spread.
Gentle sighs from nature's breath,
Echo softly, life and death.

Stars align in shimmering rows,
Moonlight melts where stillness grows.
Every gleam, a fleeting thought,
In the frost, lost dreams are caught.

Glimmers fade as dawn draws near,
Daylight whispers, soft and clear.
Yet the night will hold its tune,
In the whispers of the moon.

Untold Stories in Snowdrifts

Silent hills, a canvas white,
Snowdrifts blanket the night bright.
Each flake falls with whispered grace,
Hiding tales in winter's lace.

Footprints fade beneath the shroud,
Nature bows, serene and proud.
Voices buried in the snow,
Where only the still winds blow.

Icicles dangle, sharp and clear,
Frozen moments held so dear.
Every mound a story keeps,
In the depths where silence sleeps.

Beneath the frost, life lingers on,
In this realm, we feel the dawn.
Memory whispers, soft yet bold,
In the snowdrifts, dreams unfold.

Distant Hues of Midnight Frost

Midnight blooms in icy hues,
Whispers of the past ensue.
Crimson skies with azure veins,
Twinkling stars through frosted panes.

Each breath hangs like crystal shards,
World transformed in stardust yards.
Dreams of warmth in winter's clutch,
Painted scenes we long to touch.

Beneath the coal-black sky we tread,
In the chill, our fears are bred.
Yet we dance in shadows cast,
With each moment, hold it fast.

Translucent forms of light converge,
In the darkness, we emerge.
Frosty whispers guide our way,
Distant hues turn night to day.

Enigma of the Frozen Horizon

Endless seas of ice await,
Crafting dreams, sealing fate.
Mysteries in every crack,
Whispers linger, never lack.

Fog rolls in with secrets veiled,
On the edge, our breath is hailed.
Frosted winds bring tales from far,
Each echo, a guiding star.

Beneath the sky, a canvas vast,
Nature's beauty, unsurpassed.
Glistening shards of light collide,
In the stillness, we confide.

Puzzles wrapped in frozen charms,
Hold us close in nature's arms.
Journey forth, the heart it calls,
In the enigma, magic sprawls.

www.ingramcontent.com/pod-product-compliance
Ingram Content Group UK Ltd.
Pitfield, Milton Keynes, MK11 3LW, UK
UKHW031954131224
452403UK00010B/574